The Big Day!
Moving to a New House

Nicola Barber

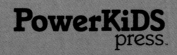

PowerKiDS press.

New York

Published in 2009 by The Rosen Publishing Group Inc.
29 East 21st Street, New York, NY 10010

First Edition

Editor: Camilla Lloyd
Designer: Elaine Wilkinson
Picture Researcher: Kathy Lockley

Library of Congress Cataloging-in-Publication Data

Barber, Nicola.
  Moving to a new house / Nicola Barber. — 1st ed.
      p. cm. — (The big day!)
  Includes index.
  ISBN 978-1-4358-2841-4 (library binding)
  ISBN 978-1-4358-2897-1 (paperback)
  ISBN 978-1-4358-2900-8 (6-pack)
  1. Moving, Household—Juvenile literature. I. Title.
  TX307.B375 2009
  648'.9—dc22

                                        2008026222

Manufactured in China

Picture Acknowledgments: The author and publisher would like to thank the following for their pictures to be reproduced in this publication: Cover photograph: Ariel Skelley/Corbis; Alan Powdrill/Taxi/Getty Images: 8; Altrendo Images/Getty Images: 7; Andy Crawford/Dorling Kindersley/Getty Images: 16, 24; Ariel Skelley/Corbis: 17; Chris Howes/Wild Places Photography/Alamy Images: 5; Comstock Select/Corbis: 15; DAJ/Getty Images: 18; Dave Cameron/Alamy Images: 9, 10; Fabio Cordoso/zefa/Corbis: 21; Horizon International Images Limited/Alamy Images: 14; Juan Silva/The Image Bank/Getty Images: 1, 6; Leslie Garland Picture Library/Alamy Images: 20; Reg Charity/Corbis: 21; Tim Pannell/Corbis: 13; Tom & Dee Ann McCarthy/Corbis: 19; Yellow Dog Productions/The Image Bank/Getty Images: 11.

Contents

Time to move

You are moving to a new house. Outside your old house, there is a sign that says "SOLD" or "FOR RENT."

What will moving be like?

Mom and Dad may have taken you to see your new house already. You might even have chosen your new room.

It is sad to leave your old house, but it is exciting to be going somewhere new.

Getting ready

Before moving day, it's a good idea to sort through your toys and games. There may be some that you would like to give away.

Your Mom and Dad help you to take down the pictures in your room. Then it's time to pack everything into big cardboard boxes.

Moving day

On moving day, the moving truck arrives early. Do you think all the furniture and boxes in your house will fit inside the truck?

The truck looks huge when it's empty.
Everything gets loaded in—even your bikes.
You can help with some of the smaller boxes.

Saying goodbye

When the moving truck is full, your old house is empty. The rooms look very odd without all the furniture. It's time to say goodbye to your old house.

You say goodbye to your friends and
neighbors, too. You can keep in touch with
your friends, and they can come and visit
you at your new house.

Staying overnight

If your new house is a long way from your old one, you might have quite a long trip.

You might have to stay overnight with friends, or maybe with your grandparents. Remember to pack your overnight clothes and your favorite toy, so that they don't go into the moving truck!

Your new house

It's exciting to see your new house. All the rooms are empty, and it feels a bit strange at first.

Soon, the moving truck arrives, and your furniture and boxes start to fill up the rooms.

It looks like a mess, but it will get better
when the furniture is in the right place and
you can start to unpack the boxes.

Unpacking

You can think about where to put your furniture in your new room. Now you can unpack your clothes and books, toys and games.

You can help your family with the unpacking
in the other rooms, too.

First night

Tonight is the first
night in your new
house. You brush
your teeth in a
new bathroom,
and go to bed
in your new
bedroom.

There are different sounds and different smells in your new house. Your parents are close by if you need them.

Exploring

Now it's time to start exploring your new neighborhood. Is there a park near your new house? Are there any stores?

Soon, you could be starting at a new school. You can make new friends, and you will still have your old friends, too.

Enjoy your new home!

Moving words

If you are writing about moving to a new house, these are some of the words you might need to use.

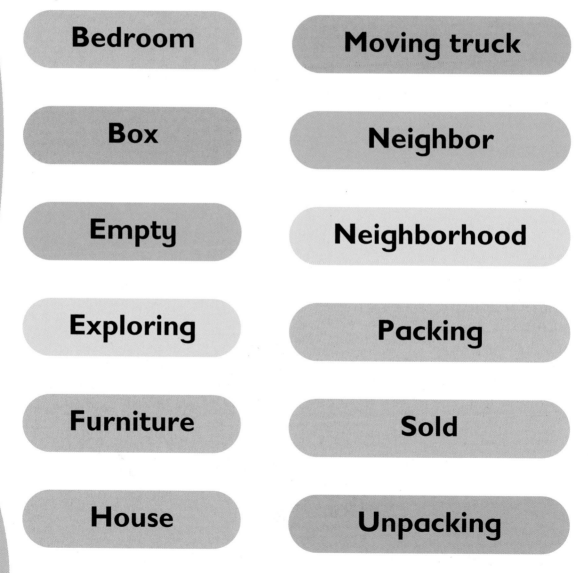

Bedroom

Moving truck

Box

Neighbor

Empty

Neighborhood

Exploring

Packing

Furniture

Sold

House

Unpacking

Further information

Books
Big Ernie's New Home: A Story for Young Children who are Moving
by Teresa Martin and Whitney Martin (Magination Press, 2006)
Lucy's New House
by Barbara Taylor Cork (School Specialty Publishing, 2002)

We're Moving (First-Time Stories)
by Heather Maisner (Kingfisher, 2004)

For parents
Moving with Kids: 25 Ways to Ease Your Family's Transition to a New Home by Lori Collins Burgan, (Harvard Common Press, 2007)

Web Sites
Due to the changing nature of Internet links, PowerKids Press has developed an online list of Web sites related to the subject of this book. This site is updated regularly. Please use this link to access this list:
www.powerkidslinks.com/bd/house

Index